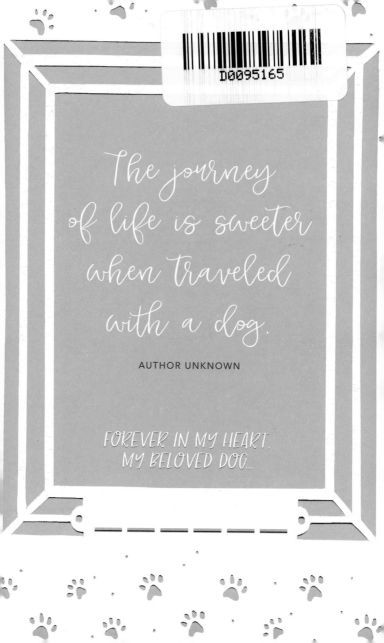

The journey
of life is sweeter
when traveled
with a dog.

AUTHOR UNKNOWN

FOREVER IN MY HEART,
MY BELOVED DOG...

Cover and interior design by Nicole Dougherty

Artwork © 2017 Ginger Chen

DOG TALES

Copyright © 2017 by Harvest House Publishers
Published by Harvest House Publishers
Eugene, Oregon 97402
www.harvesthousepublishers.com

ISBN 978-0-7369-7147-8

Printed in China

17 18 19 20 21 22 23 24 25 / RDS-JC / 10 9 8 7 6 5 4 3 2 1

DOG TALES

HARVEST HOUSE PUBLISHERS
EUGENE, OREGON

A CONSTANT COMPANION

There's nothing quite like a canine companion for unconditional love, unlimited laughs, and undeniable life lessons. We might be the ones who teach our dogs tricks, but they train us too. Raising a puppy helps us develop patience and persistence. And caring for an older dog is good practice in showing consistency and compassion.

Forever loyal, dogs definitely deserve our best.

Whether your dog is a playful puppy or a wise old four-legged friend, it's always a delight to recall the memories of your days—and years—spent in each other's company. No matter the breed, every dog has its own unique personality—and together you become the perfect pals for each other.

Have fun recalling the special moments spent with your dog—and don't worry about filling in the pages all at once. You can fill in a few pages after your daily walk, or jot down memories here and there as you reflect on your time together. (Yes, you have full permission to "dog" it!)

It's true that every dog has its day. Aren't you glad that day includes you?

A dog

IS THE ONLY THING
ON EARTH THAT LOVES YOU
MORE THAN HE LOVES HIMSELF.

JOSH BILLINGS

ALL ABOUT
MY DOG

Name

Birthdate

Breed

Eye Color

Fur Color and Type

Other Distinguishing Marks

How did your dog come into your life?
Jot down the story here.

_____

_____

_____

_____

_____

_____

_____

_____

_____

_____

_____

_____

_____

_____

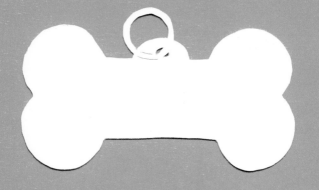

Tell the story behind your dog's name.

What brand of food does
your dog like best?

What would you consider your
canine's best quality to be?

_____

_____

_____

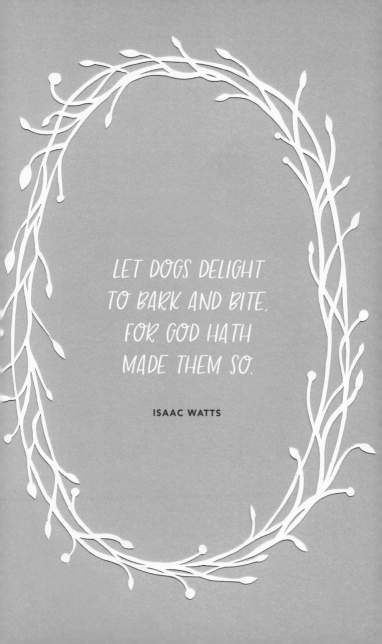

LET DOGS DELIGHT
TO BARK AND BITE,
FOR GOD HATH
MADE THEM SO.

ISAAC WATTS

Muddy feet? No problem.
Leave a paw print here.

Dogs love their toys! What does
your pup play with nonstop?

_____

_____

_____

_____

What are the top three things
guaranteed to make your dog
wag its tail with joy?

1. _____

2. _____

3. _____

Is your pup a fan of fetch or Frisbee?
Write down your dog's favorite games—
and *your* favorites!

If your dog were a song,
what would it be?

THE DOG IS THE
MOST FAITHFUL OF ANIMALS
AND WOULD BE MUCH ESTEEMED
WERE IT NOT SO COMMON.
OUR LORD GOD HAS MADE
HIS GREATEST GIFT
THE COMMONEST.

MARTIN LUTHER

What was the first thing you thought
when you saw your dog?

_____

_____

_____

_____

_____

_____

_____

_____

_____

_____

_____

_____

_____

Leaves in autumn.
Snow in winter.
Grassy lawn in spring.
Sprinklers in summer.
If your dog were a season,
what would it be?

Paste a favorite
photo of you with your
dog here.

Or take a silly selfie together now!

You can always find hope in a dog's eyes.

AUTHOR UNKNOWN

What magazine would your
dog be on the cover of?

_____

How does your dog tell you,
"You're my best friend"?

_____

_____

_____

_____

_____

Training time! What tricks have you taught your dog?

Some dogs are natural swimmers,
while others are terrified of water.
What does your pup think of the waves?

_____

_____

_____

Dogs are better
than humans
because they know
but do not tell.

EMILY DICKINSON

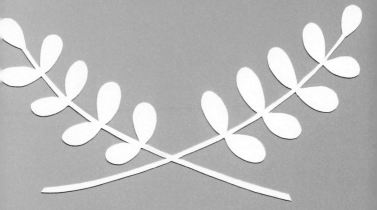

How do you spoil your dog in silly ways?

Be honest!

_____

_____

_____

_____

_____

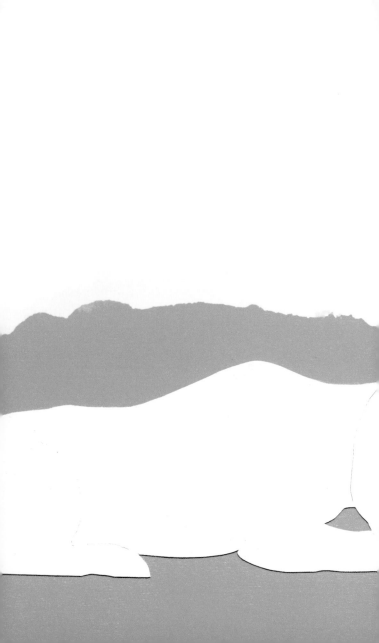

Despite their differences,
dogs and cats can be friends.
Dogs have also befriended hippos!
Does your pet have an unlikely bestie?

Dogs understand about as many words as the average two-year-old child. What words does your pet love to hear?

_____

_____

_____

_____

_____

_____

_____

Dogs have had their day all throughout literature and films. Which of these classic canines most reminds you of your cherished pet?

☐ Toto from
The Wizard of Oz

☐ Old Yeller

☐ Scooby-Doo

Disney's Pluto

Snoopy

Winn-Dixie

Lassie

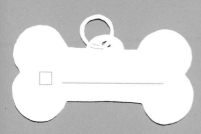

When you get out the leash,
your dog immediately knows it's
walk—or even run—time! Where do
you like to wander with your dog?

_____

_____

_____

THE GREATEST PLEASURE OF
A DOG IS THAT YOU MAY MAKE
A FOOL OF YOURSELF WITH HIM
AND NOT ONLY WILL HE NOT
SCOLD YOU, BUT HE WILL MAKE
A FOOL OF HIMSELF TOO.

SAMUEL BUTLER

Pets can give us a scare! What has
your dog done that has freaked you out?
Describe the situation—and be sure
to include the happy ending.

_____

_____

_____

_____

_____

_____

_____

_____

_____

_____

_____

_____

_____

The easy reader *Go, Dog. Go!* by P.D. Eastman features dogs driving. What kind of car do you imagine your pooch behind the wheel of?

What would your pup serve at its
favorite restaurant?

_____

_____

_____

_____

_____

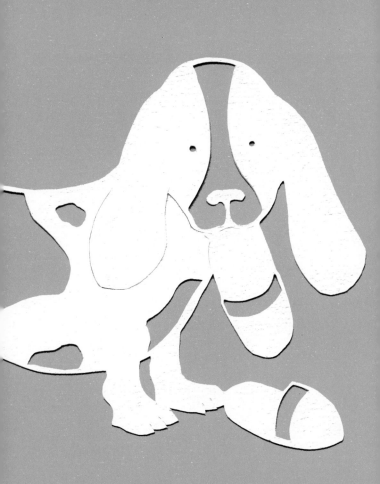

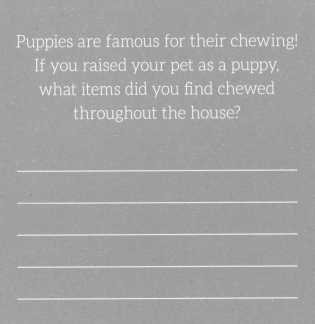

Puppies are famous for their chewing!
If you raised your pet as a puppy,
what items did you find chewed
throughout the house?

_____

_____

_____

_____

_____

How does your dog communicate that
it's happy? Unhappy? Excited? Worried?

_____

_____

_____

_____

_____

_____

_____

_____

_____

_____

_____

_____

_____

What would you title
the top three stories
about your dog's life?

1. _____

2. _____

3. _____

One
loyal friend
is worth
ten thousand
relatives.

EURIPIDES

What favorite treat does
your pup wag its tail for?

_____

_____

_____

_____

_____

Whether you're artistic or not,
make a quick sketch of your
best four-legged friend.

Doggie stick figures are totally okay!

Have you ever planned a puppy playdate? Who is your dog's favorite canine companion?

_____

IF YOU DON'T
OWN A DOG,
AT LEAST ONE,
THERE IS NOT
NECESSARILY ANYTHING
WRONG WITH YOU,
BUT THERE MAY BE
SOMETHING WRONG
WITH YOUR LIFE.

ROGER CARAS

HISTORIES ARE MORE
FULL OF THE EXAMPLES OF
THE FIDELITY OF DOGS
THAN OF FRIENDS.

ALEXANDER POPE

Describe your pup's personality
in five or fewer words...

1. _____

2. _____

3. _____

4. _____

5. _____

How does your dog communicate,
"I'm happy you're home"?

_____

_____

_____

If your dog was in a movie and voiced
by a celebrity, who would it be?

_____

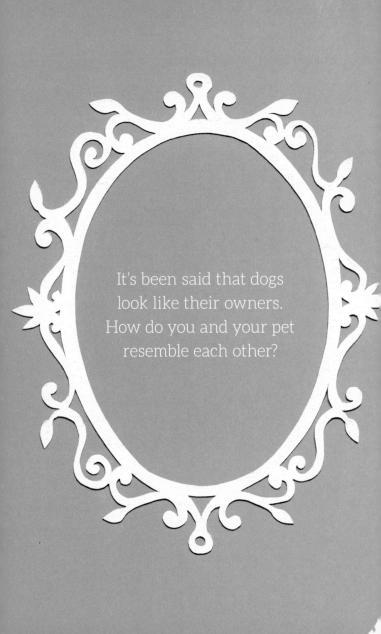

It's been said that dogs look like their owners. How do you and your pet resemble each other?

Quick—write down every silly name
you've ever called your pup.

_____

_____

_____

_____

_____

_____

If your dog were a famous person, who would it be?

What doggie park or natural area do you frequent with your pooch?

_____

Dogs instinctively know when we're feeling down. How does your canine cheer you up?

_____

_____

_____

_____

_____

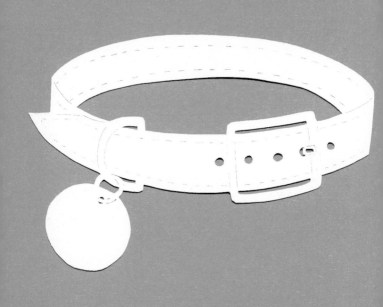

If you could dress up your dog for your favorite holiday, what would it wear?

_____

_____

_____

_____

_____

ALL THINGS BRIGHT AND BEAUTIFUL,
ALL CREATURES GREAT AND SMALL,
ALL THINGS WISE AND WONDERFUL,
THE LORD GOD MADE THEM ALL.

CECIL ALEXANDER

Dogs are big on routine. What would
your pet's ideal day include?

_____

_____

_____

_____

_____

_____

_____

_____

_____

_____

_____

_____

_____

_____

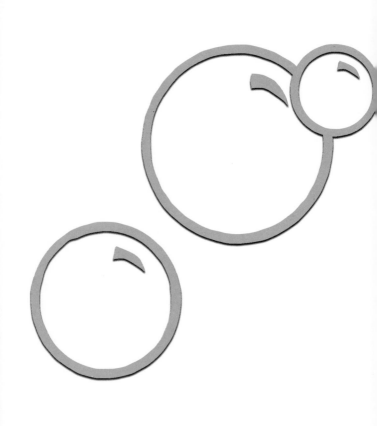

Bubbles aren't just for kids!
Blow some bubbles and record
how your dog reacts.

_____

_____

_____

_____

_____

If your dog's bark were a music genre,
what would it be?

Dogs sometimes roll around in stinky stuff. What has your canine gotten into—and how did you get it off?

_____

_____

_____

_____

_____

_____

Dogs can get distracted!
What calls to your canine
when you're out and about?

_____

_____

_____

_____

_____

Buy a pup
and your money
will buy love
unflinching.

RUDYARD KIPLING

What does your dog do when
it wants your attention?

_____

_____

_____

_____

_____

What's the weirdest thing
you've fed your dog?

_____

_____

_____

Free at last! Where is your pup's favorite place to go off-leash?

_____

THE PSYCHOLOGICAL
AND MORAL COMFORT
OF A PRESENCE AT ONCE
HUMBLE AND UNDERSTANDING—
THIS IS THE GREATEST
BENEFIT THAT THE DOG HAS
BESTOWED UPON MAN.

PERCY BYSSHE SHELLEY

What does your canine think of
car rides? Briefly, tell your most
memorable travel tale.

Some dogs are fussy about their bedtime ritual. How does your canine bed down for the night?

_____

_____

_____

_____

_____

_____

How does your pooch react when it's bath time? Jot down any crazy bathing-the-dog stories you can recall.

Nap time! Where is your dog's
prime snoozing spot?

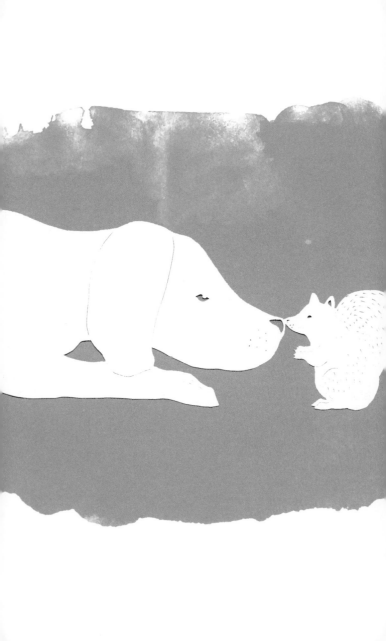

He speaketh not;
and yet there lies
a conversation
in his eyes.

HENRY WADSWORTH LONGFELLOW

How does being a dog owner
make you a better person?

_____

_____

_____

_____

_____

_____

_____

_____

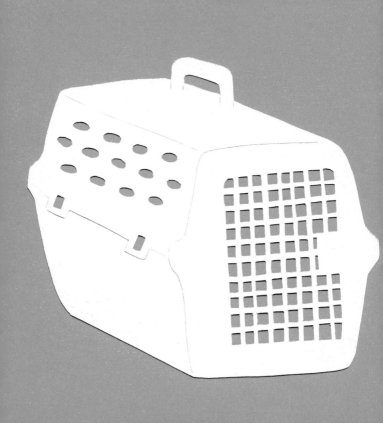

What are the top three tips you'd give a brand-new dog owner?

1. _____

_____

_____

_____

2. _____

_____

_____

_____

3. _____

_____

_____

_____

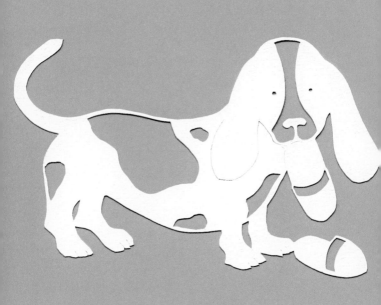

I love *this* about my dog...

Write your dog a quick note
of thanks for being such an
important part of your life.

_____

_____

_____

_____

_____

_____

_____

_____

_____

_____

_____

_____

_____

Hear our humble
prayer, O God.
Make us, ourselves,
to be true friends
to the animals.

ALBERT SCHWEITZER

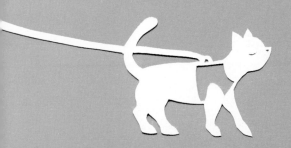

DOGGONE IT—YOU'VE DONE IT!

You've reached the tail end of the book.

And there's no need to stop here. You can return to these pages and jot down more memories and stories and fun facts. You can even start your own memory journal or keepsake scrapbook—maybe one that includes all of your dogs or other animals—using this book for ideas and inspiration.

Now, go reward yourself with a long walk or a good game of fetch or Frisbee. Take a cue from your canine and explore a new trail, savor the moment, and drink in the joy of being alive. Live out the lessons you've learned from your dog!